"BRAIN SMART"

Improving Wellbeing by Understanding Your Brain

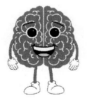

Agneta Johansson

Brain Smart: Improving Wellbeing by Understanding Your Brain

© Agneta Johansson, 2023

For permission requests, email info@Jammainternational.com

Website: Jammainternational.com

Illustrations by Alison Chusney

Edited by Kerry Laundon and Rachael Chilvers

Book production by Shamash Alidina: MindfulBookPublishing.com

Table of Contents

Testimonials

Now that I have a better understanding of how my brain works, I can rationalise my thoughts and work towards not acting on impulse or acting without thinking about what is actually happening.

Prisoner, May 2023

The Brain Smart training has helped me to be a better parent. My dad never used to talk to me about emotions, so it's not my go to. Since learning about fight, flight and freeze, I've learnt to listen more.

Prisoner and Mental Health Ambassador, Feb 2023

I am a true believer in taking things back to their roots and trying to understand the causes of why we are the way we are. It is important to understand and learn about fight, flight and freeze, and Brain Smart does this in a way that is accessible to all.

Luke, Project Lead and ex- prisoner, Un Lock My Life, April 2023

I really enjoyed the Brain Smart course and I now have an understanding of my brain's behaviour that I will take forward for life.

Nathan, Prisoner, July 2023

During Brain Smart training - I have had CBT sessions for 6 months but I have learnt more about myself in this training than in any of my counselling sessions.

Prisoner, June 2023

The Brain Smart section has vital messaging that I think everyone needs to know!

Sally – Training for Life, Trainer.

I feel like I am usually in bully mode most of the time, so now that I can identify that, I can make changes to help myself and not take things so seriously.

Young Person - August 2023

The Brain Smart training helped me to understand that I am not weird or different, and that we all go through similar things, we just need to talk about it more.

Young Person, August 2023

I didn't understand fight, flight, and freeze before, but now I feel like it is very relevant to me as sometimes I don't know how to act when bad things happen. Now I feel like I have a better understanding of myself.

Young Person , August 2023

I use Buddy Threat Mode, Bully Threat Mode, and Smart Mode in my own day-to-day life to help myself and it has definitely improved my wellbeing.

Heather, Mental Health Trainer, September 2023

I was asked to work on a collaboration with Agneta Johansson through developing her Brain & Behaviour model into a mental health and wellbeing training course, for delivery to young people in education settings in the East of England. Once this training had been co-written by my team and a group of young people who formed a project working group, we achieved clinical sign off via University College London (UCL). The training became award-winning and was subsequently re-designed to be adapted for a prison and Young Offender Institution (YOI) environment. This revised training also became award winning. The success of both of these wellbeing training models is due to the unique and groundbreaking approach to understanding our brain in a way that is both clinically user-friendly and very relatable. Agneta's thoughtful and considered approach to using her lived experience combined with evidence-based content in her writing is the key to the success that our collaboration has enjoyed and will continue to enjoy into the future.

Richard Stewart

CEO, My Life and Mental Health First Aid Instructor

.

Introduction

Imagine if you knew that there was a logical explanation as to why you sometimes feel so messed up.

Imagine if you could understand and accept that nothing is wrong with you. Yes, you may feel awful, but there's nothing wrong with you!

Imagine if you believed that you are not suffering from a disease or condition. You are not broken, just stuck with a lot of rubbish that your brain has produced. It is not your fault!

Imagine if you could learn to take control of your gloom-and-doom brain!

Our brains can mislead us into feeling that we are somehow broken. In this book, I explain how your brain creates your behaviour and your reality and I share some useful tools you can use to take control of your brain and increase your wellbeing – and turn these imaginings into a reality.

Understanding your brain

Did you know that you have a hunter-gatherer brain, which developed for conditions that existed at least 10,000 years ago when life was extremely dangerous?

Did you know that the primary purpose of the brain is to keep you safe and alive? Making you happy is not in its job description.

The human brain evolved for a life on the savannah where people lived in small groups, hunting for food and avoiding being killed by wild animals, neighbouring groups, diseases or injuries. Half of the population died before adulthood.

Today, your life is totally different from living on the savannah, but the brain hasn't changed much at all, creating a head-on collision with evolution.

Modern society presents us with new challenges. As our brains haven't evolved with the times and are still stuck in survival mode for much of the time, we can struggle to make sense of the world we live in.

Now, though we are so much safer from real physical dangers, like being eaten by a lion or killed by someone intent on stealing our food, we instead fear psychological dangers from the past or the future. At the same time, we are living with most of the world's problems in our pockets, stored in our mobile phones, which makes us worry about all the terrible things that may happen to us. Today's world can cause us tremendous stress – and our brains are not built for this level of stress. This can lead to a lot of anxiety, worry and depression.

Our way of communicating with each other has also changed. We are expected to be available day and night. Social media is another potential problem. It is great, but it can also be a curse in so many ways. We send emails and talk through apps and on the internet, which has increased the ways we can communicate but often results in people seeing and connecting with each other less in person. Online bullying has also grown exponentially.

My story

I have suffered from general anxiety for most of my life. I have also had bouts of depression. Mr Fear is often sitting on my shoulder.

I would often wonder, "What's wrong with me?" I was desperate to find something or someone that could fix me. When I was 19 years old, I decided there were only two ways to go: up or down. I chose up. I read a lot of books. Took relaxation classes. Saw several so-called specialists, but nothing really helped.

I continued my search, had years of counselling. It was good to have a hand to hold, but my anxiety and fear of living did not change.

Little did I know then that anxiety is a genetic trait that goes right back to when our ancestors were living on the savannah. The more anxious you were, the more you were alert to dangers, and the greater your chance of survival. Your anxiety (and therefore survival) would also have been good for the whole group, so you would have been a very important person!

Can you imagine the difference if my GP had said, "You are not suffering from anything but a genetic brain that is very old-fashioned and very trigger-happy. Your brain can't cope well with the world we are living in today. What you need is to learn how to control your brain." If I had learned this earlier in life, what a difference it would have made in reducing my suffering!

It wasn't until much later, when I stumbled on new research about how the brain works, that I started to realise that I was okay – it was actually my brain causing all this havoc.

Since then, I have read everything I can get hold of regarding how the brain works. I have also done a lot of different courses. All this has led to my deep understanding of how the brain creates our behaviour and reality.

At last, I started to change – to learn to drive my brain! – and my mental wellbeing greatly improved. Unfortunately, most of us don't understand how our brain can cause us so much suffering. We are often left with the feeling that something is wrong with us, instead of understanding that it is the brain's faulty programming.

Through my own personal experiences, I have developed a great interest in and passion for increasing the wellbeing of myself and others. I am now a trained counsellor and have built up a counselling department in a GP surgery. I also have trained in Acceptance and Commitment Therapy, Positive Neuroplasticity and Mindfulness and Meditation, all of which have helped to improve my mental wellbeing.

How this book can help you

Could you drive a car without having lessons? Could you cook without knowing the basics? Well, how can you control your brain if you don't understand how it works and have not learned the language to be able to communicate with it?

Plenty of books are out there that tell you how to be happy, how to stop your anxiety, how to stop worrying, how to stop your thoughts and so on. The big difference with this book is that I explain mental wellbeing from the perspective of the brain.

I want you to understand *why* your brain works the way it does, *how* this is happening and *what* to do about it.

The key to learning anything is to understand the subject. The more you understand, the more you can change. With this knowledge and the suggested skills in this book, you can choose to change.

You can become a decent cook by trying a few recipes. *But* you can become a brilliant cook by understanding how to use different ingredients to create any dish you want. You can take your learning to a different level!

You can achieve decent mental wellbeing in a variety of ways; for example, by learning a few methods to reduce anxiety. *But* you can achieve brilliant mental wellbeing by learning about the different functions of the brain, so you have the knowledge and skills to become the person you want to be.

This is why understanding the brain can be so helpful.

It is also high time to demystify psychology by doing away with 'psychobabble' – in other words, complicated psychological terms that are difficult to understand.

I want to empower you with the knowledge and skills that you should have been taught in school.

I want to help you develop the skills you need to manage and improve your own mental wellbeing.

I want you to become your own expert as I have become mine.

Becoming 'Brain Smart' has worked for me and many others I have worked with. I have a strong belief that this can also work for you.

This is pure education, not another therapy!

What you have in your hands is not a scientific textbook. Instead, this book provides you with an easy-to-follow explanation of why your brain sometimes feels like it is not on your side, and introduces you to effective skills you can use to help you take control of your brain.

Are you ready to get behind the steering wheel of your brain and take back control?

If so, please join me on the journey.

Agneta

A Note to The Reader

This book is based on all my learnings from courses, work, books, scientific papers and my own experiences.

I have chosen to simplify the subject by using the word 'brain' only rather than complicate matters by also referring to the 'mind'.

All the images of the brain in this book have happy faces to reinforce the understanding that the whole of your brain is amazing and your best friend. Your brain is doing its absolute best to protect and help you.

PART 1:

Get to Know Your Brain

In this part, I am going to help you understand how the brain works.

Chapter 1

Your Super-protector Brain: Dealing with Threats

Happiness is not in the brain's job description!

The brain has evolved to keep you safe and alive, not to make you happy.

I know this is a challenging thought – one you may not have heard before.

Of course, we have a lot of positive emotions and feelings, like happiness, joy and contentment, which is fantastic, but they are not the focus of this book.

If we did not have this extremely effective protective brain, constantly alert to danger, we would not have survived as a species. Making you feel happy has never been high on the brain's priority list.

Instead, the genetic trait to look for the negative – the danger – in situations has always been extremely important for our survival. This is called the *negativity bias*. It is better to suspect that the shadow behind the bush is a lion rather than becoming its supper!

However, a side-effect of the negativity bias is that our brains have developed a very strong tendency to look for the negative in an experience, and so we tend to see very little of the positive in the events around us.

This is less helpful today, when our lives are so much safer, but our brains are still doing it. It has been built into our genes. This is one of the brain's best weapons to keep us alive!

So, does that make you a negative person? Of course not; it's your brain trying to protect you. But with today's lifestyle this protective instinct can become a problem. The brain is still working on the assumption that it is better to be safe than sorry. This is great when the threat comes from the outside world, like being chased by an angry dog – yes, there are still many times in life when it's good to react quickly to threatening situations. But it's not so good when you're imagining that your boss is angry with you because they didn't say hello when you arrived at work.

The negativity bias is also very good at narrowing your attention and making you focus on a small negative event in a sea of many other neutral or positive events. This is another of the brain's weapons to ensure you don't miss the slightest threat of danger, however small, but it is hardly going to make your life easier if your focus is constantly diverted towards possible negative events.

For example, recently, I had a wonderful day out with one of my best friends. We did some shopping and had a great lunch. Just before going home, I had to pick up some milk. The cashier was so rude that I got really upset. What did I tell my husband about when I got home? Not about my wonderful day, but about the rude cashier! I allowed this one short event to cloud the entire day.

This is a very good example of negativity bias in full flow. It wasn't a particularly clever response, but it can happen so easily in many situations.

The brain feels it is too dangerous to let go of its protective role and focus on happiness because it could miss a threat to your safety. It doesn't mean you won't feel happy (hopefully you feel happy often!), but the brain can't help constantly scanning for danger.

Threats: Real or imagined?

How does the brain protect you from threats? By never sleeping or having a coffee break; by constantly focusing on threats, 24/7.

The problem is that not all threats are the same, even if the brain thinks so.

There are two types of threats: real and imagined. It's very important to understand the difference.

Real threats

A **real threat** is immediate and can cause bodily harm. It exists in the physical, outside world, not in our imagination.

Think about all the times you have been saved by a quick reaction to a dangerous situation; for example, quickly drawing your hand away from a hot stove, jumping back to the pavement when a speeding car comes around the corner or reaching for the banister when you stumble on the stairs.

Your survival mode activates your stress hormones, which flood your body. Your brain reacts in milliseconds, long before you've even thought about what's happening. It will hopefully get you out of danger through those instinctive reactions.

When your brain has saved the day in this way, you may have thought, "That was lucky!"

When the threat is over, you may be a bit shaken for a while, but then you are able to quickly get back to what you were doing before.

An occasional real threat produces a much stronger but shorter stress response than imagined threats, but as the brain and body are genetically adapted to cope with short bursts of real stress they rarely cause any problems.

Can you see the importance of the brain as a super-protector to keep you safe?

Imagined threats

An **imagined threat** is not imminent and cannot cause bodily harm.

These threats are from your inside world and produced by your brain and messages from your body.

They are very much dependent on our genetics (what has been passed to us through our parents and earlier generations) and our social experiences (all the experiences we have had in the past and we will have in the future).

They are usually not real, and they do not exist in the outside world. They are often fears relating to something that has happened in the past or may happen in the future.

These imagined threats are mostly illusions, fantasies or hallucinations.

They are specific to you as \a person. Someone else's fears in the same situation would be different (for example, some people have a fear of flying, while others love it).

Here are some examples of imagined threats:

- Fear of public speaking
- Believing that your boss is angry with you because you have not seen them for a couple of days
- Believing that the pain in your stomach is cancer
- Anxiety about dying from COVID
- Worrying that you are not wearing the right clothes for an event
- Feeling unloved because you haven't been invited to your friend's party
- Feeling stupid when you think someone is laughing at you

Your brain thinks there is a threat in just the same way as your brain responds to real threats. The brain evaluates this imagined threat as a danger to you and immediately leaps into survival mode.

The survival mode activates your stress hormones, which flood your body so you lose control of your attention, only able to focus on the problem. Any positive thoughts fly out of the window. It's all about focusing on the imagined risk to keep you safe.

The more you stew over the imagined threat, the more anxiety you feel. The molehill is becoming a mountain. You are now at the mercy of your brain in full survival mode. Now, you are well and truly stuck in a vicious cycle. You cannot focus on anything else. You start to feel out of control. The more you try, the worse it gets.

Thoughts arise, such as, "I can't handle this", "I want this to disappear", "I'm pathetic" and "I just want this to stop".

Not only do we imagine a lot of our own problems, but we also have a part of our brain that can't see the difference between real and imagined threats.

What has happened?

Your brain reacts in the same way to an imagined threat as it does with a real threat. The problem is that your imagined fear goes on and on until your brain doesn't evaluate the situation as a threat anymore or your fear has been resolved.

Consider the following examples of imagined threats.

You believe your boss is angry with you:

"My boss hasn't stopped by my desk for a couple of days. They must be angry with me. Perhaps I've done something wrong? Perhaps I won't get promoted? I must have done something bad. Perhaps they'll sack me?" On and on the story goes.

Or perhaps you believe that catching COVID will kill you:

"There seem to be so many people dying from COVID, so that could happen to me. Most are older or ill, but it could still happen to me. Yes, I have had the vaccination but perhaps it did not work. Perhaps my body will not cope with COVID."

On and on the story goes.

These examples show how an imagined threat can turn into a full-blown attack of anxiety.

Many of our imagined threats are more like constant background noise. We can have lots of unhelpful thoughts whirring around in our heads, driven by our fears, but they may be less threatening and cause a lower grade of anxiety rather than a full-blown attack: "Was my email correct?" "Did I look stupid when I was wearing that hat?" "Everyone else's essay was much better." "Why did I say that?" "I should have rung my friend before I left."

Sometimes we may not even be aware about our imagined threats and have a background feeling of sadness, boredom or low mood. You just have those nagging feelings of anxiety and discomfort in the back of your head that stop you from feeling comfortable and at ease.

Let's compare a response for the earlier examples with when you are not triggered by stress, so there is no imagined threat.

- "Oh, my boss didn't stop at my desk today. I do remember now; they have some important visitors and will be very busy. I am sure they'll stop for a chat another day."
- "My email is good enough; I am not pretending to be a writer."
- "I may have looked stupid in that hat, but so what? Perhaps someone got a good laugh."
- "I'm sure my essay was okay."
- "What I said may not be perfect, but I'm not pretending to be perfect."
- "Most people get good protection from the COVID vaccination, therefore I should too."

It is very easy to understand that the brain is your protector when it stops you from being run over by a car.

It is more difficult to see your brain as your protector when you are anxious about dying if you catch COVID. But it is still your brain trying to protect you.

Any time you feel threatened, whatever the reason, the brain is there to do its job. It is always on your side, protecting you from both real and imagined threats.

Most of our psychological pain and suffering stems from imagined threats.

Both types of imagined threat – that of a full-blown attack causing a higher level of anxiety or a constant background noise that causes a lower level of anxiety – can cause us problems. Even if the anxiety is less severe, it can still cause suffering and harm to our bodies.

The brain and body are genetically adapted to cope with short bursts of real stress, but they have not developed the ability to cope well with the long-term stress that imagined threats often cause. This is not good for our psychological and physical wellbeing.

How we respond to imagined threats has a significant impact on the actions we may then decide to take. Compare these two types of responses to an imagined threat:

- When you are *triggered* by the imagined threat of your boss not stopping by your desk for a couple of days, you may feel angry and decide not to do your given task to your usual high level of performance. This may lead to lots of mistakes and a poor outcome.
- When you are *not triggered* by the imagined threat of your boss not stopping by your desk for a couple of days, you continue to do the task to your usual high level of performance.

Can you see how different these responses are? When you are triggered by imagined threats, your responses and chosen actions often lead to more suffering.

Learning to see imagined threats for what they mostly are – fake news, illusions or fantasies – is the key to gaining control of your suffering.

We are all normal!

Each of us is a normal human being, struggling with a brain that still believes it is living on the savannah 10,000 years ago. It is doing its best to protect us and cope with today's modern lifestyle, but many of the brain's efforts to protect us can produce a lot of suffering.

You may have been told by a professional that you are suffering from a mental health disorder, such as general anxiety or depression. I'm sure this made you feel ten times worse!

Imagine instead this professional telling you: "Your brain is very protective and overreacts easily and this can cause you a lot of stress. Medication may dampen some of your symptoms, but the better approach is to learn how your brain works and develop some skills to help you take back some control. You are a normal human being, at the mercy of your brain's survival instinct."

What a difference! That is the professional I want to have.

(Of course, if you have any deeper concerns regarding your anxiety or depression, please consider talking to a healthcare professional.)

How can anxiety be normal? The more anxious our cave-dwelling ancestors were, the better chance they had of surviving. Anxiety kept them alert to dangers and it works the same way for us today.

How can worry be normal? Likewise, the more our cave-dwelling ancestors worried, the more likely they would have been to identify and eliminate dangers. Our brains operate the same way today.

How can depression be normal? When other tribes or animals got too dangerous, or our ancestors were suffering from disease or wounds, they would have hidden, making them more likely to survive. Today, when we feel depressed, we may withdraw, stay in bed and avoid people, a type of modern hiding.

How can anger be normal? Anger is a natural impulse that drives us into action, preparing us to fight for our lives, which was fine for cave-dwelling people, but less so in the modern world!

Having those emotions and feelings can cause difficulties. They can be truly awful. However, when you understand that these are normal responses to challenges – even lifesaving – you realise that this is completely natural, although painful. Our brain sees the world as dark and dangerous. This doesn't mean that we have bad nerves, but that we have a strong brain, which does exactly what it's supposed to do.

If we compare psychological health with physiological health, what is the difference between anxiety and a broken leg? If a broken leg is not a disorder, why is anxiety? You are just temporarily 'injured' in two different places: the body or the brain.

By understanding how the brain works, you understand that you are a normal human being and there may well be nothing wrong with you, so no disorder.

We can all change!

Your brain is programmed by the genes from your parents and your social experiences from the environment you live in. Every thought you have, every emotion, every feeling, every sensation, absolutely everything you experience, leaves a trace in your brain and affects and changes you.

The brain you have today is different from the brain you had yesterday. The brain's ability to reorganise itself by forming new neural connections throughout life is called *neuroplasticity*. You might like to think of this as rewiring your brain.

The key to getting into the driving seat of the brain is understanding how the brain works, together with learning how to change your brain through rewiring. Empowering yourself with this knowledge is a great tool for change.

The learning is easy. The challenge is to practise using these skills again and again. As we all practise negative thinking a lot of the time, we need to learn to also practise helpful thinking. Changing this strong genetic negative bias requires a conscious effort, but we all have the ability and we can do it if we choose to.

It is all about reprogramming and rewiring your brain so you can change your habits and behaviours. Unfortunately, there is no delete button. You cannot erase anything in the brain. However, with practice you can form new patterns that become stronger than the old ones. You can build new paths that take you towards how you want to be and how you want to live your life.

The question is not *if* you can change, but *how*!

When you have the understanding and the desire to change, it will fall into place, make sense and become easier.

It is important to understand that in all your struggles with life, *you* are not the problem. It is the brain's programming from our social experiences that is playing up.

But remember: you are always responsible for your actions!

Key points

- Your brain is still living on the savannah as a hunter-gatherer, and this causes a head-on collision with evolution.
- The brain's primary purpose is to keep you safe and alive.
- Being happy is great, but it is not in the brain's job description.
- The negativity bias increases your chance of survival, as you believe that life is more dangerous than it really is.
- Your brain creates a lot of imagined threats, and this can cause a lot of suffering.
- As most emotions (such as anger, anxiety and depression) have developed over thousands of years to protect you, they are vital for your survival – and very normal.
- The combination of knowledge and neuroplasticity is the key to changing your brain.
- We can all change if we know how.

Chapter 2

Understanding the Two Modes of the Brain: Threat Mode and Smart Mode

The brain constantly evaluates everything that is happening to you. This is how the brain works. With all events, all your experiences, inner and outer, the brain is always going down the evaluation path. With real threats, the evaluation is immediate and takes a shortcut, bypassing your awareness to save you from life-threatening events. With imagined threats, the brain takes a different path; it is a bit slower, so you may have some awareness of what is happening (but mostly, you don't).

The brain constantly asks whether the situation is 'bad', 'neutral' or 'good'. If the evaluation is 'bad', your brain will see it as a threat to your safety and will activate your stress system.

With imagined threats, the key to remember is that it's not the thoughts that are the problem, even if it feels like they are. It's the brain's **evaluation** of the situation that produces your thoughts; this is the problem!

It's the brain's evaluation of the situation as 'bad' that causes our difficult thoughts and our suffering.

This approach goes to the root of the problem (your evaluation) instead of trying to change the symptoms (your thoughts).

Here's an example to help explain.

You feel so hurt at not being invited to Peter's party. The brain evaluates this as 'bad'; this is a threat to your wellbeing, and activates the stress system. "Why am I not invited? There must be something wrong with me. What will my friends think? This is so horrible" – and so the thoughts go on. You are truly stuck in your horror stories. However much you try to think yourself out of feeling bad, and it may work for a short while, you still have a background noise of 'bad', as the brain has not changed the evaluation. If instead you stop and challenge the evaluation, you may start to see that there is nothing wrong with you. In fact, you might think that something is wrong with Peter for not inviting you!

So, the evaluation is the problem, but it is also the part of the solution. If you change your evaluation, you change your thoughts. If you change your thoughts, you change your outlook on life.

When you change the evaluation to 'neutral' or 'good', you will be back in the driving seat of your brain where you have control of your mental processes. (In Part 2, I explain how you can change the evaluation of a situation.)

It is very important to understand the evaluation process as it is the evaluation of an event that triggers the brain's Threat mode or Smart mode.

Understanding the two modes

We only have one brain, but to help understand the brain, I have divided it into two parts, which I call *modes*:

- **Threat mode**, which is the protective part of your brain that keeps you safe and alive.
- **Smart mode**, where the whole brain is engaged, including your thinking and reasoning.

Why do you need to understand the two modes?

Consider driving a car. You need to put petrol in the tank, you need to know how to change gear to drive at different speeds, you need to know how to brake and so on, but you don't need to understand the mechanics of each part of the car to be a skilful driver.

Likewise, with your brain, you don't need to understand the details of how it works, you just need to understand some fundamental basics – like Threat mode and Smart mode – so that you can be an effective 'driver' of your life.

If you have a driving license, you know how to drive a car. Have you been offered a driving license for your brain? Unfortunately not, but what a difference it would make if we all could learn how to drive the brain more effectively!

The more you can learn to take control of the brain, the more Threat mode and Smart mode will work in harmony and the better you will feel.

Your Threat mode

When you are in Threat mode, the brain is working very fast and powerfully, often much quicker than your thoughts. For example, it might enable you to avoid a speeding car, or it might cause you to lash out with anger towards an annoying cashier.

You are at the mercy of your brain. You can probably remember situations where you have reacted without being consciously aware, both regarding real and imagined threats.

To keep you safe and alive, your brain is constantly looking out for dangers, real or imagined. This is the job description for your brain: without Threat mode, we would never have survived as a species.

The brain uses emotions and feelings like anger, fear, disgust, sadness, surprise and so on to launch us into action. Whether the evaluation of 'bad' towards your wellbeing in a given situation is correct or not is of less importance. It is better to suspect that the strange sound in the house is a burglar than to ignore it and continue sleeping. "Better safe than sorry" is the brain's motto.

When you are in Threat mode, a real threat will produce an instant reaction, and it is unconscious. An imagined threat produces a slightly slower reaction and is conscious, even if it does not feel like it. The whole brain is now needed to use all the resources available to take you away from trouble as quickly as possible. This means that your Smart mode has been hijacked to help you get out of trouble.

You cannot stop, think and plan if a car is speeding towards you. That would probably mean certain death. In such situations, we are very grateful for the brain's ability to make super-quick decisions.

Do you stop and think before lashing out in anger? Probably not. Even if in theory we could stop and think, we mostly don't. At times like these, we may be less grateful for our brain's ability to react in a quick way.

In Threat mode, stress hormones are released, prompting us into a fight, flight or freeze response (also known as attack, avoid or shutdown):

- **Fight:** for example, feeling anger or rage; blaming; being aggressive or shouting.
- **Flight:** for example, feeling anxious or overwhelmed; wanting to get out of the situation; skipping work or classes; withdrawing.
- **Freeze:** for example, feeling overwhelmed or numb; hiding from the world; struggling to make decisions.

With stress hormones racing through our bodies, we can only focus on the threat. The brain requires all our attention to keep us safe and alive.

When your Threat mode is activated, the brain becomes very powerful and trigger-happy, with the sole purpose of looking out for dangers. It presumes danger is present until it is convinced otherwise.

There are no coffee breaks and no time to sleep. The brain is working day and night.

Threat mode has two parts: it is a **Buddy**, in that it can save us from real dangers, and yet at the same time it can be a **Bully** and cause us a lot of suffering.

Threat mode as your Buddy

Threat mode as a Buddy is what kept our ancestors alive and enabled the survival of our species.

The Buddy has become a super-protector for the human race. We are the survivors and the descendants of the fittest!

Today, of course, this super-protector is still helping us to stay alive, even though the types of dangers are very different from those of our ancestors; they are much less frequent and less deadly. But we still face risks, so we can be very grateful for the Threat mode and the way it acts as our Buddy.

Recently, I came back from Sweden where they drive on the right-hand side of the road. When I arrived back in the UK, I had to do some errands and walked down to town. I was deep in thought while trying to cross a road. The problem was that my brain was still in Sweden. I was looking in the wrong direction. I heard a loud car horn and I instinctively jumped back to the pavement.

Thanks to my Buddy, I got away safely.

Threat mode as your Bully

Our lives have changed so much from the time we lived on the savannah 10,000 years ago. We are so much safer and most of us live to a ripe old age. The real threats have decreased dramatically.

The problem is that with the life we live today, we have so many imagined threats and they can cause a lot of suffering, and with those threats the Bully is in control.

Another problem is that our stress system has not evolved to cope with this level of stress. As a result, it causes a lot of strain on our mental and physical health.

So, how are a lot of us living today?

- We live in big cities crammed with people.
- We absorb a lot of the demands and pressures from our surroundings.
- We engage with social media that shouts at us to be happy, smart, rich, beautiful and so on.
- We compare ourselves to others.
- We experience bullying, which has grown exponentially due to social media.
- We struggle with our mental wellbeing, which we see as a fault with us rather than understanding it from the perspective of the brain and evolution.
- We are told by professionals that we are suffering from mental disorders and many doctors dish out pills like sweets.

I am sure you can come up with many more examples of ways we live today that aren't especially helpful and can have a negative impact on our wellbeing.

Of course, taking medication is very valuable in certain situations, and so is getting help from professionals. However, with a lot of our more day-to-day suffering, there are other ways to help ourselves, such as by learning how to drive the brain.

The way in which we live today has led to plenty of imagined threats. They are not the real threats coming from the outside world, but the threats that come from your Bully. Gosh, how some of these imagined threats can make life troublesome. Stress from worrying about taking a test, being late for a meeting, feeling stupid in a class, thinking we have been rejected by friends and so on. Life has changed so much, but our brain is mostly still functioning as if we are living on the savannah.

The Bully provides a non-stop, one-way monologue in your head. Maybe it tells you how stupid you are or generates thoughts that undermine you. For example, "Why did I say that?", "I am a failure" or "I am so stupid."

For a lot of us, this becomes how we live our lives. Our worries, fears, jealousy, insecurities and so on take over our lives, and you feel lost or overwhelmed. Are you telling yourself that you can't live like this any longer? Are you constantly reminded about risks and how dangerous different situations are? You might start to feel you are living in a never-ending nightmare, but the brain is just doing its job.

Threat mode can't tell the difference between a real danger (such as a growling dog running towards you) or an imagined danger (such as believing you are going to fail an exam). So, all those threats are activated in the brain in the same way.

When you are in the grip of the Bully, you are switching between living in the future and the past, never really in the present. If we take the example of worrying about failing an exam, the horror story you are telling yourself could be: "I know I'm going to fail the exam; I'm not so clever. My parents think I'm messing up most of what I do. If I don't pass, I'll have to redo the year. What will my friends think of me?" – and so the story goes on. Are those thoughts going to help you to be in the best shape for the exam? Probably not! Being the best version of yourself or making important decisions is almost impossible when you are in the grip of the Bully.

Are you in control of your brain or is the brain in control of you? If your Threat mode is activated, then the Bully is in charge.

It is uniquely human to create stories based on snippets of information and our previous experiences. We are so convinced that the stories we tell ourselves are real, but most of them are useless and destructive, although we often don't realise it.

What makes the situation worse is that the more you believe your imagined stories, the more stressed you become. The more you try to control your thoughts, the more powerful and elaborate your fantasies become.

This is not how we should be living!

We have many thousands of thoughts a day. According to Dr Fred Luskin of Stanford University, a human being has approximately 60,000 thoughts per day, and 90% of these are repetitive! As we are also genetically programmed towards negativity (for survival purposes), a great number of our thoughts may not be to our advantage.

The Bully is not concerned with being correct; it takes the approach of 'better to be overprotective than make a mistake', so you can easily understand how many opportunities there are every day for being bombarded with threatening thoughts and feelings.

Try to remember that the whole of the Threat mode (Buddy *and* Bully) is designed to keep you safe and alive. Think of it as a guard dog that attacks everyone who comes into your home. It doesn't do so because it is a bad dog! It just wants to protect you. We need to train it to see the difference between a friend and a foe.

Your Smart mode

When you realise that there is no threat to your wellbeing or survival, either by having changed your evaluation of the threat or not being triggered, you will be in Smart mode. The evaluation of the situation is either 'neutral' or 'good'. Now you have access to the whole brain.

When you are in Smart mode, you are in control of your cognitive functioning. Here is where your reasoning, problem-solving, comprehension, impulse control, creativity, perseverance and emotion regulation are taking place.

You can recognise this mode easily when whatever you are doing is running smoothly and you feel good. You are responding to life without feeling threatened.

For example, you are in Smart mode when you are spending a day out with some friends and fully enjoying yourself; you're at work and focused on the task at hand; you're doing housework and feeling at ease and happy with finishing a boring task; you're feeling content in whatever you are doing, with no negative, repetitive thoughts about the past or the future.

When you are in Smart mode:

- You can see the whole picture of a situation from different perspectives.
- You can use your creativity.
- You can think and come up with ideas.
- You can reason, plan and find solutions.
- You can feel empathy, love and compassion.
- You can live in the present.

- You can calmly think about the future.
- You can decide the kind of person you want to be.
- You can decide how you want to feel and the life you want to live.
- You can look back at the past in a neutral way, choosing to feel regret or think of what you can learn from past events.
- You can ponder on happy or sad memories.

And so much more.

In Smart mode, you can look at your imagined threats and investigate if they are true. For example, the Bully may be telling you, "I am so stupid," but if you shift into Smart mode you may tell yourself, "Why am I telling myself this? I know I am so much more." Or the Bully may be telling you "I can't do this," while in the Smart mode you may tell yourself, "I know I am good at so many things, so why do I put myself down?"

In Smart mode, your general outlook in life, in whatever you are doing, will be much wiser and this will affect everything you do and how you feel.

In Smart mode, you can decide who you want to be, how you want to function and if you are going to keep telling yourself those negative statements. Or you can choose to discard them and instead tell yourself how good you are (while at the same time not expecting yourself or anyone else to be perfect).

In Smart mode you are living in reality, with no imagined stories, and you're free from threats. It is this mode you want to be in as much as possible. In this mode, you are no longer at the mercy of your Bully.

Our brain is a fantastic organ as long as we are not hijacked by the Bully. Look at how we have developed as human beings and made the world what it is today. Everything we have come to rely on has been created because of our wonderful brains: mobile phones, cars, the internet, medicines and flying to the moon, to name just a few.

Who is in the driving seat, Threat mode or Smart mode?

Who is running your show? If it is your Threat mode, ask yourself: "What are the stories the Bully is telling you, what movie is running and what role are you playing?" The brain is an expert storyteller and loves focusing on risks. However, if there is no threat to your wellbeing, you are in Smart mode.

You can imagine it as a switch that is constantly flicking between the two according to what is happening. Where is the switch now?

As we know, the Threat mode springs into action as soon as we get triggered by a real event (a car speeding towards us) or imagined event (worrying that we might be sacked). In both cases, we lose control over our thinking and reasoning.

Speed is the Threat mode's secret weapon – it's great if we have to jump out of the road to avoid a speeding car, but not so helpful when we have imagined the story about getting sacked.

When we are hijacked by the Threat mode, we are blind to reality. We only see from the eyes of the threat. It is like having tinted glasses, coloured by fear.

So, how do we clear our glasses and see who is in the driving seat?

We need to wake up – to stop and become aware of what is going on, and who is driving the brain. We need to take back control of the steering wheel, return to Smart mode and take constructive actions to help us live a more vital and purposeful life. (For more on taking action, see Part 2 of this book.)

It is in Smart mode where you can see the illusions, fantasies and stories of the Bully for what they are: imagined threats. Here, you gain awareness of what is going on. Your fear-coloured glasses are clearer; you are waking up from your nightmare. What freedom!

The more we practise, the stronger we become.

With knowledge, we have a choice.

With skills, we know how.

We can make different choices at different times.

**We can choose to stay the same,
or we can choose to change.**

The first step towards gaining this essential awareness is to check if you are where you want to be.

Am I thinking – in Smart mode?

OR

Are my feelings thinking for me – in Threat mode?

Getting into the habit of asking yourself this question is key. It is helpful to do so regularly, whether that is daily, hourly or minute-by-minute.

Remember that whatever you are feeling is totally normal. It is part of being human.

Everyone has a tricky, trigger-happy brain that works this way – even the wisest people, like the Dalai Lama.

Nothing is wrong with you. You did not design this way of being – your genes did.

But remember that you are always responsible for your actions.

We all have a choice

Do you want to continue the well-trodden path you have taken for years where your brain has been mostly in control? Or do you want to be in charge and live the life you want?

It may not always feel like we have a choice, especially when we have been hijacked by Threat mode. But when we understand what is happening, we do have a choice – we can start along the path towards having more control over and freedom from our Threat mode.

The more you choose to practise, the freer you become – and *this* is your choice.

With the right knowledge, understanding and skills, you can take over the steering wheel and drive your brain in a new direction.

Key points

- You need to learn how to drive your brain in the same way as you need to learn how to drive your car.
- It is the brain's evaluation of an event as 'bad' that needs to change for you to have fewer difficult thoughts and better wellbeing.
- Your Threat mode with the Buddy and the Bully are always on your side to keep you safe, although it may not feel like it when you're hijacked by the Threat mode.
- With real threats from the outside world, your Buddy is in charge. With imagined threats from your inside world, it is the Bully in charge.
- In Smart mode, you are free from imagined threats and have full access to your amazing brain.
- Ensure that you regularly check in with yourself to see which mode you are in.
- You are free to choose the Threat mode or the Smart mode – the choice is always yours.

Chapter 3

Understanding Your Emotions and Feelings

Your emotions and feelings are the brain's alarm system.

Your emotions and feelings are not your enemy, even if this is how it can feel sometimes. They are there to warn you of risks to your safety and wellbeing. Understanding when they are useful and when they are not can be of tremendous help.

We have both positive and negative emotions and feelings, but in this book, we are focusing on the negative feelings that can cause us so much suffering.

Emotions are the brain's reaction to real threats

The brain has evolved over thousands of years, but for most of this time people have been living as hunter-gatherers experiencing many life-threatening events. Our emotions are the brain's alarm system, so they had to become very well developed and extremely sensitive. Only the most vigilant people survived. Our emotions are an important tool in helping our brains push us to take the right actions.

The emotions that come from *real threats* produce the fight, flight or freeze response. Here, our Buddy is in full swing. These responses are unconscious and are immediate and not within your control. For example, while walking home in the dark, if you suddenly hear a noise that frightens you, your *freeze* mode is automatically activated, so you freeze on the spot – the brain needs time to evaluate the situation. If the brain is not able to make sense of the noise, the *flight* mode may be activated, so you might turn around and run back to where you came from, but your *fight* mode may also be activated, so perhaps you quickly grab your handbag to use it as a weapon, ready to lash out. If the brain can make sense of the noise – maybe it's just a car backfiring – you continue walking.

Examples of emotions from real threats are sadness, fear, anger, surprise and disgust, and they are *unconscious*, which is different from feelings that are mostly conscious (more on this in the next section).

A lot of people want to get rid of difficult emotions, but we can't. They are the brain's alarm system, and without them we would not stay alive for long.

Feelings are the brain's reaction to imagined threats

How are feelings different from emotions? They differ from person to person and are very much due to our social experiences. Feelings are also a part of the brain's alarm system, but here, the Bully is in full swing with 'imagined threats'. They are not immediate (even if they feel so) or life-threatening, but they can be very problematic. They can produce the most amazing and wild stories. An example could be: "If I go to the party in the wrong clothes, I will look like a fool; I will be a laughingstock, and people will think I'm stupid; friends won't want to see me again." Is this a threat to your safety? No, this is not a real threat to you.

By knowing how to change your feelings, by changing your brain's evaluation of a threat being 'bad', you can shift back into Smart mode and look upon the situation with totally different eyes. Perhaps you will instead tell yourself, "Is there any such thing as the wrong or right clothes? And if someone has a problem with my clothes, it is their problem!"

Feelings are much the same as emotions, like anger, anxiety, worry, hate, sadness and so on, but the big difference is that feelings *are mostly experienced consciously*. If you stop, take a deep breath and ask yourself, "What is happening?", you can recognise the whirlwind of your feelings.

Trying to get rid of or suppress your feelings is not a good idea; even if they feel awful, they may have an important message.

Because feelings are mostly experienced consciously, you can choose to challenge the ones that cause you suffering, get into the driving seat of the brain and start to take back some control (for more on taking action, see Part 2 of this book).

Remember:

- Emotions are unconscious, come from real threats from the outside world and cannot be controlled.
- Feelings are mostly conscious, come from your inside world (your brain and your body), and can be challenged and changed.

What emotions and feelings have in common is the stress response and how we experience them – as anger, fear, worry, sadness, disgust, grief and so on.

Did you know? Your feelings are powerful enough to influence your thoughts and behaviours, yet according to neuroanatomist Jill Bolte Taylor, this influence only lasts physiologically for 90 seconds at a time. Just let that sink in... 90 seconds. If you do not feed your feelings with stories, they will disappear.

The brain is a storyteller

Your brain is a fantastic storyteller. With its amazing imagination, it would easily get the first prize in any storytelling competition.

Everything we think, remember and experience turns into stories. The brain builds stories so it can remember details of events. All our experiences with our individual interpretations become our unique story, and what is important for the brain is stored in our memory. As the stories differ from person to person, there are as many stories about each event as people involved. You can see how difficult it is to decide which story about an event is true and explains what really happened.

The brain never stops working in the same way as your heart never stops beating. You may not always be consciously aware of your stories, but they are always there. The brain is always looking out for dangers, even when you sleep, to keep you safe and alive. It is very difficult, if not impossible, to stop having stories, and the more we try, the worse it gets. They have a life of their own!

What happens with your story-making when the Bully, together with your imagined threats, is in control? The stream of stories turns into a stream of epic movies. To make it worse, you are playing the main role and all the action is about you. See how easy it is to get hijacked by the brain?

When you watch a movie, you become totally absorbed. You get frightened, excited, sad and so on. When you stop watching, you know that it was not a real event. It may have felt real, but you know it was temporary entertainment.

However, we are often not aware that the personal, imagined movies we create are not real: we don't wake up to the fact that they are, most of the time, the brain's imaginings. And to make it worse, we blindly believe what our brain is telling us – it feels very convincing and completely real, and we take it as fact!

You can see how imagined movies can cause us big problems. You live in it for minutes, hours, days. For some, it may never end.

As the brain never gets tired, we can live in one nightmare after the other. The Bully loves to ask, "What if this happens, and this, and this?"

Why is the brain making up all those stories? It seems like madness! As it is the brain's task to keep us alive and safe, it *must* find a solution to get us out of a potential threat.

The best way for the brain to do this is to imagine as many stories as possible relating to the situation and to find solutions to them. Therefore, we are bombarded by this constant chatter of worries and anxieties. Having your Bully sitting on your shoulder babbling away is definitely not a good place to be in.

Here comes the next problem! We cannot think ourselves out of an imagined threat – it is impossible. You may get rid of the stress for a short time, but it will come back later. You need to get out of the nightmares by changing the evaluation of 'bad' so you can get back into Smart mode and the driving seat of the brain. Now you can find much more helpful and constructive solutions.

Remember: don't be angry with yourself or your brain, that will just make it worse – the brain is doing its best to protect you.

Consider the Native American parable of the two wolves.

The Tale of the Two Wolves

One evening, an old man told his grandson about a battle that goes on inside every person.

He said, "The battle is between two 'wolves' inside us all. One is evil. It is anger, envy, jealousy, sorrow, regret, greed, arrogance, self-pity, guilt, resentment, inferiority, lies, false pride, superiority and ego.

"The other is good. It is joy, peace, love, hope, serenity, humility, kindness, benevolence, empathy, generosity, truth, compassion and faith."

The grandson thought for a minute and then asked his grandfather "Which wolf wins?"

The old man replied, "The one that you feed."

Why can't I avoid my thoughts and feelings?

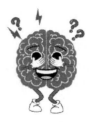

Oh, how wonderful it would be if we could avoid all thoughts and feelings arising from our difficulties. It can seem so tempting and easy to avoid different people or events in life. But will it work? Yes, it may work in the short term, but these tactics have a habit of coming back to haunt you and also to become worse. Sometimes it can even become a phobia. Your feelings are telling you that something may be wrong and needs to be investigated.

Perhaps you avoid public places for fear of having a panic attack, or say no to a job for fear of public speaking, or avoid going through parks for fear of seeing dogs, or avoid going to parties for fear of social settings.

Yes, they are brilliant techniques for now. But avoidance just makes it worse in the long run.

Why is that?

By avoiding thoughts and feelings from the situation, you are still sending the messages of danger to the brain. The evaluation of the situation is still 'bad' and as long as this is the case, the Bully will keep you under lock and key.

The brain's evaluation is also reinforced each time you avoid a situation, and if this continues to happen, the worse the fear will become. The path in the brain that starts as a small trail may develop into a motorway. You now have the 'danger' truly fixed in place, which makes it more difficult to change.

If you are perceiving an imagined threat, you need to challenge the brain's evaluation of 'bad'. In Part 2 of this book, I explain how you can find a new and much more constructive way of dealing with your feelings while gaining improved mental wellbeing in the process.

Key points

- Your emotions are unconscious and function as an alarm system to warn you of real threats and to guide you into action. They cannot be controlled.
- Your feelings are mostly conscious reactions to your imagined threats and can be challenged and changed.
- Your brain loves storytelling and makes up fantastic stories about imagined threats, which are so easy to believe.
- Avoiding thoughts and feelings is like putting your head in the sand – it just creates more and stronger threats.
- The more you try to think yourself out of difficult thoughts or feelings, the deeper your fear and suffering will become. It is only by changing your evaluation of 'bad' that you will change your thoughts and feelings.

PART 2:

How to Drive Your Brain

In this part, I am going to help you get back in the driving seat of your brain.

Chapter 4

Discover New Skills to Change your Evaluation and Rewire Your Brain

Imagined threats need to be challenged, as most of the time they do not exist in reality and so are not true. We need to develop the skills of unhooking from the imagined threat and seeing the perceived threat for what it is – an illusion. When we return to Smart mode, we can see reality again.

The following five steps are based on skills that will gradually change the evaluation, help you to shift back to Smart mode and can be used anytime you realise you are in Threat mode.

You need to work through these steps in order.

As with everything we learn, in the beginning it takes time, but with practice it will become easier.

I suggest taking 5–10 minutes for the steps at first. Start by writing down your responses. (Engaging the language centre in the brain is another skill and it will help you detach from the Threat mode.)

When you get the hang of it, you'll be able to do the steps in a minute or two, with no need to write down your responses.

The five steps can become a tool in your pocket to use anytime and anywhere:

- Stop
- Observe
- Describe
- Investigate
- Absorb your success

1. Stop

If you feel stressed or anxious, the brains alarm bell is ringing. When you **Stop**, it will help you to become aware of a potential threat.

This is the first step towards realising that the Threat mode's alarm system has been activated by an evaluation of a situation as 'bad' and a threat to your safety.

WHY do you need to stop?

We so often function without the awareness of what we are doing or thinking, on so-called autopilot. Life just goes on being controlled by our brain. We have to make a conscious effort to 'wake up' from this stage. To learn to get out of autopilot, we need to first stop. If you need a way of reminding yourself, perhaps put a Stop sign on your fridge door or as a screensaver on your phone; anything that will help you remember.

This is the first step towards becoming aware that you are triggered.

2. Observe

When we feel overwhelmed or shocked, it can be really hard to start to shift out of our Threat mode.

Yes, there may be a problem that needs to be resolved, but it will help to first feel more stable and grounded by observing what is okay before we start to change the evaluation. If we can observe what is working well in our lives and appreciate some of what is okay (or even great!), this will help us to put our negative feelings in perspective. If we can also see some of the good things in life, this will hopefully make the imagined threat look a little less important. It will then be easier for us to shift from the Bully part of our Threat mode to our Smart mode. And when we are in Smart mode, we are much better equipped to deal with a potential problem in a constructive way.

In this step, you **Observe** what is working well and appreciate what is okay in your life. For example:

- I am alive
- I have people I care about
- I have food in the cupboard
- I have lots of friends
- I have a home

(Please choose phrases that work for you.)

Doing some deep-breathing exercises can also help you shift out of Threat mode.

Try this simple, helpful exercise:

1. Breathe in, counting to four as you inhale.
2. Hold your breath – for the count of four.
3. Breathe out, counting to six as you exhale.

Repeat for as long as you like.

Breathing out relaxes the stress system, so it is important that the out-breath is longer than your in-breath.

WHY will this help?

Observing what is working well in your life will help to break the focus on being totally absorbed in the threat. The breathing exercise will start to calm your stress system down. Both of these exercises will help you to see more of the whole picture of your life.

Focusing on what is good in your life is always a good skill to practise at any time in your life and is the second step towards freeing your Smart mode from the grip of the Bully.

3. Describe

When you are in the Bully part of your Threat mode, you are often not aware of your reactions to the stories you are being bombarded with. Your brain is on autopilot, and you don't really know what you are thinking and doing.

By naming or writing down your thoughts and feelings (in other words, you **Describe** them), you become more aware of the stories the Bully is telling you.

It is very important to do this step in a detached, neutral and non-judgemental way. Remember, if the Threat mode smells danger, you are vulnerable to being hijacked.

Try these phrases to help you get started:

- My Bully is telling me.....................
- Here we go again. Hello anxiety, you are telling me.....................
- There are feelings of.....................

By doing this, you shift away from feeling that you are personally worried or anxious, and towards seeing that the Bully is telling you that you are worried or anxious. It's nothing to do with who you are; it's only your Bully screaming.

- "I am stupid" changes to "My Bully is telling me I am stupid."
- "I am going to fail my exam" changes to "Here we go again. Hello anxiety, you are telling me I am going to fail my exam."
- "I am nervous" changes to "There are feelings of nervousness in my body."

Can you see the difference?

WHY will this help?

Describing what the Bully is saying ("There are feelings of..." or "My Bully is telling me...") shifts your thinking so you become more detached from your thoughts and feelings (and so less hijacked by them). Why is this important? Because you describe something about you as if you are talking about something or someone else. You can now start to see the imagined movies the brain is playing, rather than seeing yourself at the centre of this imagined threat. You are not blindfolded anymore. This gives you a chance to see how unrealistic and false the movies are and change the evaluation.

Also, when you are triggered by stress, your ability to use language is weakened. By putting words to the thoughts and feelings, you slow down the stress response and it becomes easier to see how wrong your thoughts and stories may be.

You have started to question the evaluation and taken another step towards freeing your Smart mode from your Threat mode.

4. Investigate

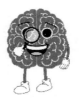

In the Describe step, you shifted from saying "I am stupid" to "My Bully is telling me I am stupid." Now you are ready to investigate if what the Bully is telling you is really true and find alternative and more constructive ways of talking to yourself so you can start to challenge your evaluation.

Consider the following questions when evaluating the threat:

- "Is this a threat to my safety?"
- Your answer may be, "No, it is not; I am perfectly safe."
- "Is this a real threat?"
- Your answer may be, "No, it is made up by my Bully."
- "On a scale of 1 to 100%, how true is it?"
- Your answer may be "2%".
- "Is it in my best interests to be hijacked by these imagined stories?"

- Your answer may be, "No, this is definitely not in my best interests, there are so many other things I could do instead."
- "Is this all that I am?"
- Your answer may be, "No, I am so much more than my Bully's horror stories!"

I am sure you can find more statements to challenge your evaluation.

By asking these questions you will come up with much more realistic and helpful statements. The goal of **Investigate** is to change your evaluation from 'bad' to 'neutral' or 'good', and this will release your Smart mode from the grip of your Bully. This is the only way to stop the alarm system of the Threat mode – it gets bored!

Now you can say to yourself:

Hurrah! I am back in Smart mode. Well done, I am fantastic!

WHY will this help?

You are now challenging the evaluation by investigating if it is really correct. Remember, it is the evaluation that produces your thoughts and feelings. The way to change how you think and feel is to change the evaluation. Now you can see clearly what your Threat mode (with its imagined threats) is up to.

As soon as there are no more threats, your Smart mode is free and you can respond in a much more helpful way.

Questioning what your Brain is telling you is a very valuable skill for you to learn and use at any time in your life, and is the fourth step towards freeing your Smart mode from your Threat mode.

5. Absorb your success

When you have changed the evaluation from 'bad' to 'neutral' or 'good' and come back to your Smart mode, you have made a huge change. Congratulations!

According to American psychologist Rick Hanson, you can also reinforce your reprogramming of the brain through positive neuroplasticity. This means to really feel your success, in your whole body if possible. Say it out loud, and feel the joy from your achievements. You can also write them down. Express your success in these ways as often as you wish. The more you do this, the more you will rewire your brain.

Consider some of the questions from the Investigate step:

- On a scale of 1 to 100%, how true is it? Imagine your answer is 2%. You can tell yourself, "Hurrah! I'm 98% safe, fantastic!"
- Is this a real threat? You can tell yourself, "Hurrah! this is fake news, I am okay."

With most of the questions, you can also finish with a general statement, such as:

"Hurrah! I'm back in Smart mode."

Make your own list of useful statements that helps you to '**Absorb your success**' and repeat them as often as you like.

WHY will this help?

These useful statements will reinforce the rewiring of your brain.

The more success you 'absorb', the more your brain will rewire in a positive way, and the greater the improvement in your outlook on life will be. You will see more of all the positive experiences you have that have been hiding behind your genetic tendency to focus on the negative ones.

Say to yourself:

"For each positive statement of success I absorb, I'm becoming stronger and better at driving my brain. Hurrah!"

Key points

- **Stop:** Alarm bells are ringing. Stop and realise that you are triggered.
- **Observe:** Consider what is good in your life. Breathe deeply.
- **Describe:** Name the experience: "My Bully is telling me…"
- **Investigate:** Ask yourself, "Is this a threat to my safety?"
- **Absorb your success:** Say a useful statement out loud to reinforce the rewiring of your brain.

Use these key points as a reminder. Perhaps put them on your phone, have a card in your pocket or put the reminder on the fridge; whatever is best for you.

Chapter 5

Meeting Your Co-drivers: Acceptance and Self-compassion

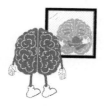

As well as the five steps explained in Chapter 4, you can invite two powerful co-drivers to help you stay in the driving seat of your brain – **acceptance** and **self-compassion**.

Acceptance

When we are in the grip of the Bully, practising acceptance can feel very wrong and is probably the last thing we want to do. How can we accept something that make us feel so bad?

Acceptance is often misunderstood, so I want to take some time to explain what I mean by acceptance. This knowledge can help you free yourself from the Bully, change your evaluation, get into the Smart mode and take more helpful actions.

When the Threat mode is fuelled by the evaluation of 'bad', we are bombarded by difficult stories that produce two different types of negative feelings in relation to the event:

1. We experience negative feelings *from* our personal reactions to the imagined threat aspect of the event.
2. We have negative feelings *towards* the event itself.

Consider this example from Peter. "James was shouting at me in front of my friends – he said, 'How can you be so stupid?' I am absolutely fuming with anger – now my friends will think I am stupid (an imagined threat), how dare he."

The first type of negative feeling is Peter's personal negative reaction arising *from* the imagined threat aspect of the event: that James is making Peter look stupid in front of others.

The second type of negative feeling is Peter's negative feelings of anger *towards* the event itself: the behaviour of James.

Splitting these two types of negative feelings apart can be so helpful when it comes to getting into your Smart mode.

If you can focus on your personal negative feelings *from* your reaction to an imagined threat (here, that Peter feels James is making him look stupid), you can then start to follow the five steps in Chapter 4 to change the evaluation from 'bad' to 'neutral' or 'good'. It is only through accepting your difficult thoughts and feelings – acknowledging that your personal reaction to the event is not a threat to you – that you can change the evaluation and stop the Bully from continuing to *perceive* a threat to your wellbeing.

Accepting your personal feelings is not the end goal, but a necessary way to shift you into Smart mode. From this point, you can then look upon the negative feeling you have *towards* the event (here, Peter would look at his negative feelings of anger about James's behaviour) in a calm and constructive way, and decide what actions to take, if any. You are now in the driving seat of your brain and can make smart decisions.

If you do not first accept your personal negative reaction *from* the imagined threat aspect of the event, and take a moment to change the evaluation, you may react out of anger because you are in Threat mode, which may lead to a totally different action (and probably not a helpful one) than if you first return to Smart mode.

Seeing the two different parts of the event and dealing with them separately is a much more healthy and helpful way to respond to difficulties. Responding to a difficult event when you're hijacked by the Bully is not going to be helpful for you or help you handle the event.

For example, I was in a restaurant with a very good friend. The waitress was very rude, and I got angry. "How dare she? We are guests, she is destroying our evening, shall we leave and go somewhere else?" the story of my Bully (the imagined threat aspect) went on. Now, my negative feelings *from* my personal reactions to the waitress being rude were in full swing. Storming out of the restaurant would not be a helpful or pleasant experience for me and or for my friend.

Then I remembered the acceptance skill. I told myself, "I have a choice to give her my power and let her spoil our evening, or I can accept that I am angry and not feel threatened about it." I went with the second choice. I called the manager and politely asked for another waitress. After that we had a great evening. Having used the acceptance skill, I could get back to the Smart mode and deal with the negative feeling *towards* the event. My anger had gone and I felt powerful, and I did not embarrass myself or my friend by striking out in anger.

Later on, the first waitress came to our table and apologised, explaining she had had some bad news and wasn't on top form.

Acceptance doesn't mean that you like what is going on or you are giving in, or that you're not going to do anything about a difficult situation. Sometimes you will choose to take action, and sometimes you will choose not to. You can only make wise decisions when you are in Smart mode.

Accepting your negative feelings, your personal reactions *from* the event, even if they feel horrible, tells your brain, "This is not a threat to my survival. Move back to Smart mode, where I can, if needed, make helpful, productive decisions."

Accepting difficult feelings, in all sorts of situations, as a normal part of life is the best way to avoid them becoming worse or becoming blown out of proportion. We do not need to like them, but we do need to accept that they exist.

Feelings can feel very scary, but they cannot hurt you.

Self-compassion

Compassion is important for survival. Thousands of years ago when we lived on the savannah, having the empathy to care for each other and ourselves was a part of staying safe and alive. If you could not feel compassion and help your tribesperson or yourself in need, you would threaten the survival of the group and become a weak link. This could lead to you being pushed out, and that would mean a sure death.

But what is compassion? Compassion is the ability to relate to someone's suffering and want to help them. So, how do we do this? By being kind and non-judgemental, giving encouragement, and if possible offering help. Compassion also helps us accept people for who they are, forgive their mistakes and be happy for their success.

Self-compassion means to turn compassion inwards and be compassionate towards ourselves. When we are self-compassionate, we are kind, understanding and non-judgemental towards ourselves, and we give ourselves encouragement and support, instead of being self-critical, unkind and angry with ourselves when we think we have made a mistake.

According to American psychologist Kristin Neff, self-compassion increases our happiness, optimism, curiosity and connectedness in life. It also decreases our anxiety, depression, rumination (getting stuck in negative thinking) and fear of failure.

Not only is it right to care for yourself, but being kind and compassionate towards yourself will also help you choose more helpful actions towards yourself, other people and your surroundings.

Self-compassion is a genetic trait, a survival tool meant to be used, and it can help you to take better actions. It's great to have self-compassion in your pocket to increase your resilience in life.

So, as we are born with this genetic ability to care for ourselves, why are we not so good at it today?

- Our self-compassion is very much dependent on our life experiences: how have we been brought up, how have we been treated by significant others and how has life in general treated us?

- We may have been socially conditioned to feel little self-compassion as it is often seen as being egoistic or self-centred.
- If you were criticised a lot as a child, you are probably not telling yourself how wonderful you are but instead are self-critical.
- You may feel you are not worth self-compassion. Perhaps you have been judged to be a bad or difficult person. This is wrong. Self-compassion is a survival tool as it helps us all to make better choices in life, hence giving us a greater chance of staying alive.

Perhaps an example will help to clarify.

I once accused a friend of mine, in front of others, of lying about me. Later I discovered that this was not true. This set off my Bully big time: "Why did I do that? I am so stupid, everyone will hate me, I am a bad person."

After practising the five steps described in Chapter 4 and reminding myself that self-compassion helps with accepting yourself, and also helps you to make wiser decisions, I chose to feel kindness towards myself and my struggles: "I accept that I am just another human being who makes mistakes like everyone else. I am not perfect. I will keep practising and hopefully think with my Smart mode before I react next time."

Now, being in Smart mode, I could look at the event and see my part in it. I told myself, "I am okay, but what I did was not okay. I chose a bad action." This shift made a huge difference, as I could then take responsibility for my actions without negative feelings towards myself continuing to whirl around me, and I was able to deal with the situation in a much more constructive way.

Can you see the difference? There are so many difficult events in our lives where we choose to be unkind towards ourselves or others. But am I a bad person? No, but maybe my actions are not always wise. If you don't feel threatened, you have the ability to make better choices and also look upon situations as potential learning experiences. Of course, it is not only when we have chosen a less constructive action that we need to be kind to ourselves and our struggles. We can choose to always feel kind towards ourselves!

Accept that you will make mistakes. Your actions will sometimes disappoint yourself and others. You may fail or make a fool of yourself. This is all part of learning and growing. It is all part of being human. We all do it!

Your weaknesses are also your strengths. Without them, you cannot feel empathy for yourself and others. Great! You are a balanced human being!

Let go of the illusion that you or anyone else can be perfect. Perfection is neither normal nor desirable. It's an illusion. We are all normal human beings, warts and all.

Here are some sentences you can use to practise the skill of self-compassion. Choose the sentences that relate to you or make up your own. Repeat them often to help you feel good about yourself and your success. This will help you to grow self-compassion and change your brain.

- My mistakes just show that I am growing and learning.
- I deserve compassion, tenderness and empathy like anyone else.
- I am not the only person feeling this way; most people do.
- I am patient with myself.
- This is an opportunity for learning – I am not a failure.
- I am the most important person in my life.
- I value myself.
- I accept myself, warts and all. It is okay to make mistakes.
- How would I treat a friend in a similar situation? I can apply this to myself.
- We are all normal, just in different ways.

You can also practise the 'Absorb your success' step from Chapter 4 by experiencing the good feelings from your achievements, and really feel the kindness towards yourself in your body.

Key points

- The more we can accept our personal negative feelings, the more we can be in Smart mode and the better we can deal with the obstacles on our path.
- The kinder we become towards ourselves and our struggles, the more helpful and constructive actions we can take.
- Self-compassion is genetic and a survival trait. We are all meant to be compassionate to ourselves as well as others.

A Final Reflection

It is our brain that creates
our behaviour and reality!

We need to get to know this amazing creator and learn to communicate with the brain so that we can become the best version of ourselves and have improved mental wellbeing.

In a nutshell, the more we live in Threat mode, the more we live in an illusion – so the more we will suffer; the more we live in Smart mode, the more we live in reality – so the more awareness, wisdom and mental wellbeing we will have.

I hope that this journey has given you enough understanding and skills to get into the driving seat of your brain.

I hope that this journey has enabled you to start to take responsibility for your own wellbeing and continue your journey in the best way for you.

I hope that taking you on the journey of my understanding of the brain will help you as much as it has helped me and many others.

I wish you all the best!

From your fellow traveller,

Agneta

About the 'Brain Smart' Programme

My passion is to design life skills programmes to build capacity and resilience in people where everyone, no matter their financial situation, can learn to improve their wellbeing. I have developed the programme in this book (*Brain Smart: Improving Wellbeing by Understanding Your Brain*). It is a programme for everyone, no matter their age or capability. I believe that to master your wellbeing, you don't need complicated information, techniques or language; instead, you simply need to be empowered with knowledge about how the brain works so you can develop your ability to manage your brain. This should be a human right. Empowering people with knowledge enables them to become their own healers and improve their mental wellbeing. This 'Brain Smart' programme is being used by mental health charities and has become part of the curriculum in some schools. It is also being developed for prisons.

Printed in Great Britain
by Amazon